Restaurant Catering Multipliers

The 17 No Cost Laws of Catering Sales Growth

by
Michael Attias

www.CaterZen.com

$19.50
ISBN 979-8-218-48695-2
51950>

9 798218 486952

TABLE OF CONTENTS

4

INTRODUCTION

RESTAURANT CATERING MULTIPLIERS

Yesterday I had a consult call with a pizzeria franchisor interested in helping her franchisees increase catering sales.

She asked me the silver bullet question, "Where can I get a list of all of the catering buyers in our markets?"

The short answer from me, "There is no silver bullet. The list does not exist. Someone has to call each business to find the qualified catering buyers."

The long answer is another book.

Nothing takes the place of selling and hustling. My most successful catering clients all have one thing in common: someone sells!

I didn't generate over a million dollars a year (2005 sales when I sold) from ezCater, Google Ads and my good looks. Every day I was hustling to close catering sales.

For those of you who lack the motivation to sell or to hire someone to sell, let me
offer a list of seventeen no-cost strategies to sell more catering.

Though not a silver bullet, consistently applying this list will result in noticeable catering sales growth...

unless your food and service suck.

In that case, nothing will help you.

In full disclosure, everything on my list is built into our catering software, but you can do it all yourself without our software.

CaterZen just makes it simple and provides an all-in-one solution.

Now onto my list and more catering sales for you!

CHAPTER 1
PROPOSALS THAT SELL

CHAPTER 1

Alright, folks, let's get down to business. Back in the day, I didn't have the luxury of fancy software tools. I was just a guy with a dream and a lot of hustle.

My catering proposals were crafted using Word and Excel, and I put everything I had into making them as compelling as possible.

You see, a proposal isn't just a list of services and prices—it's a chance to make a killer first impression and show potential clients why they should choose you over the competition.

The Impact of a Professional Proposal

Think of your proposal as a first date. You want to put your best foot forward, right? A clean, professional, and visually appealing proposal can set you apart.

It's not just about the content but how you present it.

I remember including everything from cover graphics to testimonials and even pages of pictures highlighting different catering options. These weren't just fillers—they were strategic tools to upsell and cross-sell.

One of my clients, using our templates, found that a simple page full of vibrant photos often prompted clients to order more than they initially planned.

Why Looks Matter

People are visual creatures. A polished proposal with a clean design and well-organized information not only looks good but builds trust.

It says, "We are professional, we care about our presentation, and we'll do the same for your event."

Research indicates that using high-quality images and a professional layout can boost conversion rates by as much as 30%. This means that a well-crafted proposal can significantly increase your chances of closing a deal.

Personalization

Customization is key. Whether it's a personalized cover letter, a tailored menu, or including a section of FAQs, these details make clients feel special and understood.

It's like speaking directly to them, addressing their specific needs and concerns.

During my early days, this approach helped me secure repeat business and build long-term relationships with clients.

Affordable Tools

When I started, I didn't have all these digital tools. I had to hustle—manually crafting proposals, delivering them personally, and following up diligently. This hands-on approach taught me the importance of every detail.

My hard work paid off, with my catering business growing to over a million dollars a year.

Today, you have so many affordable options at your fingertips. Canva, Google Slides, even PowerPoint—use these to create beautiful proposals. The important thing is to keep your branding consistent and your message clear.

Remember, it's not about being the cheapest option; it's about offering the best value.

Wrapping Up

Your proposal is more than just a document—it's your story, your promise, and your first step toward building a successful catering business. A polished, professional proposal sets you apart, but don't forget that following up is equally crucial.

It's often the difference between a lost opportunity and a new client. In the next chapter, we'll delve into the art of following up on proposals, exploring strategies that can help you convert more leads into loyal customers.

CHAPTER 2

FOLLOW UP ON PROPOSALS

CHAPTER 2

Let me tell you something, folks: "The fortune is in the follow-up." This mantra has been my guiding star ever since I started in the catering business.

You've put in the work to craft a beautiful, professional proposal, but if you think your job ends there, think again! Following up is the key to turning potential clients into paying customers.

QUOTE REMINDER

Subject Line:	Quote Reminder	
Type:	Call	
Assigned to:	Jeanne Summers	Call Center A
Due Date:	In 1 week	9:30 AM
Reminders:	1 hour before	

On Aug 16, 2024 , Meagan T Smith with CZ created a $3,417.99 Quote for 19 people from 11000 Roosevelt Boulevard Philadelphia, PA 19116 location. Quote # : 196176

Cancel   Create Reminder

Why Follow-Up is Crucial

How many times have you called a business for a quote, only to hear crickets afterward? It's frustrating, right?

The same goes for your clients. If you don't follow up, you're not just leaving money on the table; you're sending a message that their business isn't important to you.

Back in the day, I was relentless with my follow-ups. I remember one client who was on the fence about choosing our catering services for a big corporate event. I followed up with a personalized email and then a phone call offering a free tasting session.

That little extra effort not only secured the deal but also led to a long-term business relationship with regular repeat orders. It's all about showing clients you care and are willing to go the extra mile to meet their needs.

The Psychology of Follow-Up

Following up shows that you're committed and professional. It reassures clients that you're interested in their event and ready to help make it a success.

A well-timed follow-up call or email can significantly increase your chances of closing a deal. In fact, 60% of customers say no four times before they finally say yes, highlighting the importance of persistence   .

Moreover, businesses that follow up with leads quickly—within five minutes—are 100 times more likely to convert them.

Tactics for Effective Follow-Up

1. **Set Reminders:** A simple calendar reminder can ensure you never miss a follow-up. For larger events, offering free tastings or site visits as part of the follow-up process can provide a tangible experience of your service, which often seals the deal.
2. **Personalize Your Approach:** Tailor your follow-up based on the client's needs and the specifics of their event. Mention details from your previous conversations to show you've been paying attention.
3. **Use Multiple Channels:** Don't just rely on one form of communication. Use a combination of phone calls, emails, and even texts if appropriate. The key is persistence without being pushy.

The Cost of Not Following Up

Imagine spending hours crafting the perfect proposal, only to let it gather dust because you didn't follow up. It's like dropping the ball at the one-yard line.

Research shows that a lack of follow-up can result in losing up to 80% of potential sales, as most sales are made after the fifth follow-up.

Simply put, if you're not following up, you're not closing deals.

Wrapping Up

Following up on proposals isn't just a nice-to-have; it's an essential part of your sales process. It's the difference between a lost opportunity and a new client.

So, set those reminders, make those calls, and don't stop until you get that "yes." Next, we'll explore how re-booking reminders can keep your calendar full and your business thriving.

CHAPTER 3
RE-BOOKING REMINDERS

Alright, let's talk about one of the simplest yet most powerful tools in your catering arsenal: re-booking reminders.

Now, back in my early days, I didn't have fancy software to keep track of events and clients. But that didn't stop me from creating a system that worked like a charm.

After each large event, I'd photocopy the catering sheet and slip it into a file folder labeled from January to December. This was my "tickler system," and it was a game-changer for securing repeat business.

The Power of the Tickler System

Why was this method so effective? Well, it's all about timing and being proactive.

RE-BOOKING REMINDERS

As the new year approached, I'd pull out the folder, review the events from the previous year, and start making calls.

This way, I could reach out to clients before they even thought about booking their holiday parties or corporate events with someone else.

It wasn't sophisticated, but it was incredibly effective. This no-brainer and super-simple strategy brought in tens of thousands of dollars in repeat catering sales each year.

One year, after a particularly successful holiday season, I sat down and photocopied each catering sheet, diligently filing them away. By October of the following year, I started going through the files, making calls.

One of my calls was to a corporate client who hadn't yet planned their annual holiday party. Because I reached out first, not only did I secure that year's event, but I also upsold additional services, adding a significant boost to the overall sale.

This simple system kept my business top-of-mind for clients and prevented them from looking elsewhere.

Consistency and Reliability

Clients appreciate reliability and attention to detail. By using a system like this, you're showing that you remember them and value their business. It's not just about getting a booking; it's about building a relationship.

The tickler system made it easy for me to touch base with clients at the right time, offering them exclusive options and early booking discounts, which they loved.

The Modern Approach

Today, there are more efficient ways to handle this, especially with tools like CRM systems that can automate reminders and track client interactions. However, the principle remains the same: stay ahead of your clients' needs.

Even if you're working with manual processes, the key is to be organized and proactive.

The Cost of Forgetting

Imagine your clients as spinning plates. If you don't keep them spinning with regular touchpoints, they'll fall.

Not using a re-booking reminder system is like letting those plates drop. According to sales studies, up to 80% of future revenue comes from 20% of existing customers.

Failing to re-book these clients not only loses immediate sales but can also harm long-term relationships and brand loyalty.

Wrapping Up

Whether you're using a manual tickler system or a high-tech CRM, the principle is the same: don't wait for your clients to come to you. Be proactive, stay organized, and keep those relationships strong.

Next, we'll dive into the importance of customer feedback and how it can be a goldmine for improving your catering services and increasing customer loyalty.

CHAPTER 4

MYSTERY SHOP PHONE CALLS

CHAPTER 4

Let's get real for a moment—your phones are probably the weakest link in your catering business.

It's not just about answering calls; it's about how those calls are handled.

Back when I first opened my restaurant, I took a bold step and mystery-shopped my competitors via phone, posing as a catering buyer.

What I found was shocking.

From kitchen workers who could barely speak English to managers who asked me to call back later, and even answering machines—each call felt like I was dealing with the sales prevention department rather than a sales team.

The Importance of Mystery Shopping

Mystery shopping isn't just about spying on competitors; it's a vital tool for assessing your own business's performance. Over the years, some of my consulting clients have asked me to mystery shop their phones. Most of them failed miserably.

The truth is, only those trained to take catering calls should be handling them. A missed upsell or a frustrated prospect can cost you tens of thousands of dollars in lost catering business each year.

Observations and Best Practices

For restaurants who cater, phone interactions are often the first point of contact with potential clients. This is where first impressions are made, and they last. One common issue is that the person answering the phone isn't adequately trained to handle catering inquiries or to make upsells effectively.

This lack of training can lead to missed opportunities and lost revenue.

Tools for Monitoring

Whether you're using a simple telephone mic or the more sophisticated phone recording system in CaterZen Catering Software, monitoring what happens on your catering phones is crucial.

These tools help you listen in on calls, review them, and identify areas for improvement.

It's not just about catching mistakes; it's about training and refining your approach to ensure every call is handled professionally and effectively.

CHAPTER 4

The Cost of Poor Phone Service

You might think that one missed upsell or a single unhappy caller isn't a big deal, but it adds up.

According to industry data, poor customer service interactions can lead to a loss of up to 20% in potential sales. That's a staggering amount, especially when you consider that the catering industry thrives on word-of-mouth and repeat business.

A single bad experience can ripple out, affecting not just the customer in question but their entire network.

Wrapping Up

Monitoring and improving your phone service isn't just about catching mistakes; it's about creating a seamless, professional experience for your clients. It's the difference between being just another option and being the preferred choice for catering.

In the next chapter, we'll explore how to leverage feedback from these interactions to fine-tune your services and increase customer satisfaction.

MYSTERY SHOP PHONE CALLS

CHAPTER 5

UPSELLS: ONLINE ORDERING, PHONES & FORCED OPTIONS

CHAPTER 5

How would you like to increase your catering sales by 10-20% instantly? The strategy to employ is upselling. It's a simple yet highly effective way to boost your revenue with minimal effort.

When done right, upselling can significantly enhance the profitability of your business, especially through items like drinks, desserts, upgraded entrée and side choices, and extra sides.

These items are often high-margin, making them excellent targets for upselling.

The Power of Upselling

Upselling isn't just about pushing extra products; it's about enhancing the customer's experience by offering them more value. For instance, when customers order a catering package, they might not immediately think about adding drinks or desserts.

However, with the right prompt, many customers appreciate the option and choose to enhance their order. This approach not only increases the total sale but also improves customer satisfaction by providing a more complete catering experience.

UPSELLS: ONLINE ORDERING, PHONES & FORCED OPTIONS

Practical Approaches

Upselling can be effectively implemented through simple yet strategic prompts. For example, after a customer selects their main dishes and sides, a prompt asking, "Would you like to add a dessert to complete your meal?" can be highly effective.

This method, commonly used in various sales settings, encourages customers to consider additional purchases they might not have initially planned.

Online Ordering and Upsell Modules

Does your online ordering interface have an upsell module built in? If not, you're missing out on a significant opportunity. Our system can include forced options that act as upsells. For example, when a client

Some Special Offers for You

No thanks, I just want to complete my order >>

Cookie Platter

Would you like to add a Cookie Platter to your Buffet? Receive 10% off the Cookie Platter!

Includes an assortment of cookies: chocolate chip, oatmeal raisin and snickerdoodle presented in a platter along with tongs.

Accept this Offer Now >>

🛒 Your Order

10	Pizza Buffet	$8.99
	- with Pizza Choices (Thin Crust Veggie)	
	- with Pizza Choices (Thin Crust Cheese)	
	- with Pizza Choices (Thin Crust Sausage Crumble)	
	- with Buffet Salad Choice (House Salad)	

	Subtotal	$89.90
	Tennessee Sales Tax: (9.25%)	$9.56
	Gratuity	$13.48
	Total	**$112.94**

Add a coupon code

Proceed to checkout

orders a catering package, the system can prompt them with an option like a dessert item.

This gentle nudge ensures that upselling opportunities are not missed, as customers must actively decline additional options, making them more likely to consider adding them.

Forced Options

Forced options ensure that customers are presented with all available add-ons, such as premium side dishes or desserts. Even if a customer declines, being prompted to make a choice increases the likelihood of them considering these options in the future. It's a simple yet effective way to boost sales without being overly aggressive.

Implementing Upsells in Manual Processes

Even without sophisticated technology, upselling can be integrated into your sales process. If you are using a paper order form, include upsell questions directly on the form. For example, have a section that asks, "Would you like to add a beverage package?" or "How about some of our delicious desserts?"

Requiring a Yes/No response ensures that the question

is always asked, increasing the chances of a positive response.

Wrapping Up

Upselling is a straightforward yet highly effective strategy to boost your catering sales. Whether through online systems or manual processes, the key is consistency and training. Make sure your team is equipped and encouraged to offer these additional options to every customer.

Next, we'll explore how gathering and leveraging customer feedback can further refine your services and drive business growth.

CHAPTER 6

DETAILS/NOTES
ON CLIENTS

CHAPTER 6

In the catering business, building strong relationships with your clients is a cornerstone of success. It's not just about providing great food; it's about creating a seamless and personalized experience. We all want to do business with those we know, like and trust.

One powerful way to achieve this is by keeping detailed notes on each client. Whether it's a favorite dish, a food allergy, or a special occasion, having this information readily available makes you not just a vendor, but a valued business partner.

The Importance of Client Details

Imagine you have a regular corporate client who always orders lunch for their team meetings. You know the company president has a gluten allergy, and you've noted this down. Every time they place an order, you make sure to include a gluten-free option. This attention to detail makes your client look like a hero to their team and ensures they keep coming back to you.

It's these little touches that set you apart from competitors who might not take the time to remember such specifics.

DETAILS/NOTES ON CLIENTS

Tracking Client Preferences

Keeping track of your clients' preferences, special requests, and even past issues they've had can be invaluable. It shows that you care about their experience and are committed to making every event perfect.

This information can be stored in various ways, from old-school note cards to sophisticated CRM systems. For instance, our highlighted notes feature in the CRM allows you to see important client details at a glance, whether you're reviewing a client's history or taking a new order.

Using Client Information Effectively

Not only does keeping detailed notes help in providing excellent service, but it also opens up opportunities for upselling and personalized marketing. Knowing that a client often orders a certain type of cuisine can help you suggest new menu items they might enjoy.

CHAPTER 6

If a client has frequently ordered for corporate events, you can offer them special packages or discounts for their next big event. This personalized approach can significantly boost client loyalty and repeat business.

Practical Steps for Keeping Client Notes

1. **Choose a System:** Whether it's a digital CRM or a physical filing system, choose a method that works for you and stick with it. Consistency is key.
2. **Capture Key Details:** Focus on collecting relevant information like dietary restrictions, favorite dishes, preferred service styles, and past feedback.
3. **Update Regularly:** Make sure to update the notes after every event or interaction. This keeps your records current and useful.
4. **Make It Accessible:** Ensure that everyone who interacts with clients has access to these notes. This way, the client experience remains consistent, no matter who they speak with.

Wrapping Up

In the catering industry, attention to detail and personalized service can set you apart from the competition. By meticulously keeping detailed notes on your clients, you ensure every interaction is smooth, personalized, and professional.

DETAILS/NOTES ON CLIENTS

This builds stronger relationships and fosters repeat business.

Next, we'll delve into offering invoicing and house charges, exploring how providing flexible payment options can enhance client convenience and loyalty.

CHAPTER 7

OFFER INVOICING/ HOUSE CHARGES

Let's talk about a topic that many caterers shy away from: offering invoicing and house charges. No one likes the idea of lending money, especially when it comes to waiting for payments or, worse, dealing with collections.

When I managed my million-dollar-a-year catering profit center, we routinely had around $25,000 in outstanding accounts receivable. That's a significant amount, but it also represents a key aspect of serving our clients better.

The Benefits of Offering Invoicing

Offering invoicing isn't just about being lenient with payments; it's about making life easier for your clients.

Catering buyers often have to navigate internal processes to get a credit card approved or a check cut. By offering terms, you're removing these hurdles, making it more convenient for them to do business with you.

And let's face it, all things being equal, a catering buyer will often choose the caterer who offers flexible payment options.

Enhanced Client Convenience

Providing the option to pay via invoice can be particularly appealing to corporate clients who may prefer or require billing and invoicing for their records. This flexibility can set your business apart, making you a preferred vendor.

While it involves some risk, with proper management, the benefits often outweigh the drawbacks.

CHAPTER 7

Financial Considerations

Extending credit does come with risks, such as the potential for bad debts. However, in my experience, these risks can be mitigated with a robust system for monitoring accounts receivable.

Moreover, offering invoicing and house charges can often be cheaper than credit card processing fees, especially when factoring in the cost of borrowing working capital.

Implementing Invoicing and House Charges

If you're considering implementing invoicing, here are a few steps to get started:

1. **Set Clear Terms:** Determine your payment terms—Net 30, Net 45, etc. Make sure these are clearly communicated to your clients.
2. **Use Technology:** Utilize software solutions to automate invoicing and payment tracking. This reduces manual errors and streamlines the process.
3. **Monitor Accounts Receivable:** Keep a close eye on outstanding invoices and follow up promptly. This helps maintain cash flow and minimizes the risk of bad debts. CaterZen offers a monthly system that automatically emails aging reports to clients with

outstanding balances. These reports have hyperlinks to the actual invoices with ability to print, save a PDF version or click to pay by credit card.

4. **Offer Multiple Payment Options:** Give clients the flexibility to pay by check or credit card. This can enhance their experience and increase the likelihood of prompt payment.

Wrapping Up

Offering invoicing and house charges is a strategic decision that can enhance client loyalty and convenience. While it involves some risk, the benefits often outweigh the drawbacks, especially when managed properly. It not only provides clients with flexibility but also positions your business as a professional and accommodating partner.

CHAPTER 8

ORDER CONFIRMATION (DAY BEFORE)

We've all been there. Your driver shows up with a catering order, only to be met with confusion and the dreaded line, "I called and canceled the order earlier in the week. I spoke with a woman."

More often than not, the client can't remember the name of the person they supposedly spoke to, leaving you with wasted food and wasted time. This situation is not only frustrating but costly.

The Importance of Order Confirmation

To prevent such scenarios, it's crucial to confirm all catering orders the day before the event. This simple step can save you from unexpected cancellations and gives you a chance to make last-minute adjustments or upsells. Whether you do this through a phone call or an email, confirming orders ensures that both you and your client are on the same page.

Avoiding Miscommunication

Confirming orders helps avoid costly mistakes and misunderstandings. It's a way to double-check that all details are correct, from the time and location to the menu and any special requests. This proactive approach not only protects your business from unexpected cancellations but also enhances the client's confidence in your professionalism.

Opportunity for Upselling

An order confirmation call or email isn't just about confirming the details; it's also an opportunity for upselling. You can use this time to suggest additional items that the client may have forgotten.

For instance, you could say, "P.S., if you forgot to order your dessert or drinks, please call now or reply to this email." This gentle nudge can lead to increased sales and a more complete experience for your clients.

Implementing a Confirmation Process

1. **Set a Standard Procedure:** Establish a clear procedure for confirming all orders the day before. This could include a script for phone calls and a template for emails.
2. **Train Your Team:** Ensure that all team members understand the importance of this process and are trained to handle it efficiently.
3. **Use Consistent Communication:** Whether through phone calls or emails, make sure the communication is clear, friendly, and professional.
4. **Document Everything:** Keep records of all confirmations and any changes or additions made.

This documentation can be invaluable in resolving any disputes.

Wrapping Up

Order confirmations are a crucial step in ensuring smooth and successful events. They prevent costly mistakes, provide a chance for upselling, and reinforce your professionalism.

ORDER CONFIRMATION (DAY BEFORE)

CHAPTER 9

DELIVERY
COMMUNICATION

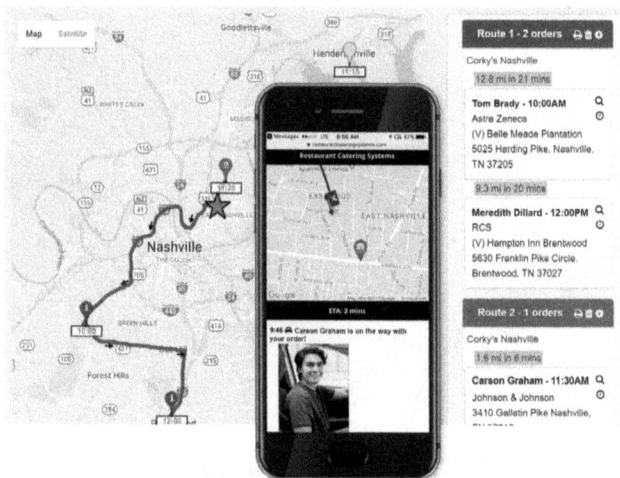

Remember the days before Uber? Calling a taxi was like playing a game of roulette—you never knew if the cab would show up within twenty minutes or two hours later. This uncertainty made planning nearly impossible.

Then Uber came along, and with a simple app, you could see your driver in real-time, knowing exactly when they'd arrive. This innovation eliminated a major pain point for many.

The Importance of Delivery Communication

In the catering world, effective delivery communication

is just as crucial. Are your drivers letting clients know when they're on the way? Are they providing accurate estimated delivery times?

With today's technology, there's no reason to leave clients guessing. Apps like Waze and Google Maps give drivers precise ETAs, allowing them to communicate this information clearly to clients. This transparency can significantly reduce the stress associated with wondering, "Where's my order?"

By keeping clients informed about the status of their delivery, you not only meet their expectations but also exceed them, turning what could be a potential point of frustration into a positive experience.

Using Tools for Communication

Even if you're not using specialized delivery software, there are still plenty of tools available to ensure effective communication. For example, standard messaging apps or even simple phone calls can be used to keep clients updated. The key is consistency and reliability—make sure that your drivers are trained to provide updates and that they have the tools they need to do so efficiently.

The Value of Real-Time Updates

Providing real-time updates is more than just a courtesy; it's a competitive advantage. In an era where clients expect transparency and instant communication, being able to provide accurate updates on delivery status can set you apart from competitors.

This is especially true for large corporate orders, where timing and coordination are critical. By offering real-time updates, you give your clients peace of mind, ensuring they know exactly when to expect their delivery.

Building Trust and Loyalty

Consistent and clear communication builds trust with your clients. When they know they can count on you for timely and accurate updates, they're more likely to become repeat customers.

This level of service is a key differentiator in the catering industry, where client relationships and reputation are everything.

Practical Steps for Implementation:

1. **Train Your Team:** Ensure that all drivers are trained to communicate effectively with clients, including

providing ETAs and updates on any delays.

2. **Standardize Procedures:** Develop a standard procedure for communication that includes when and how drivers should provide updates.

3. **Leverage Available Tools:** Use tools like GPS apps and messaging systems to facilitate communication. Even a simple call or text can make a big difference.

4. **Gather Feedback:** After implementing these procedures, gather feedback from clients to continuously improve the communication process.

Wrapping Up

Effective delivery communication is a key factor in providing an outstanding client experience. By keeping your clients informed every step of the way, you not only reduce their anxiety but also build a stronger relationship and encourage repeat business.

CHAPTER 10

NICHE MARKETING - WORKING WITH CLIENT GROUPS

I'm a big believer in the saying, "The riches are in the niches."

Within your catering client universe, there are hidden niches with untapped sales potential. Targeting these specific groups can lead to significant business growth and increased profitability.

The Power of Niche Marketing

Niche marketing is about identifying specific segments within your broader client base and tailoring your marketing efforts to meet their unique needs and preferences.

This targeted approach can be more effective and efficient than general marketing because it speaks directly to the interests and needs of a particular group.

NICHE MARKETING -
WORKING WITH CLIENT GROUPS

Real-World Example

At my restaurant, we used niche marketing practically every month. One of our most successful strategies was Black Friday mailings to major retailers.

By focusing on this specific group, we landed anywhere from $6,000 to $12,000 in single-day catering sales. This success came from understanding the needs of our niche—retailers who wanted to treat their staff during the hectic shopping season—and delivering a targeted message that resonated with them.

Using CRM for Niche Marketing

A good CRM (Customer Relationship Management) system is essential for effective niche marketing. It allows you to categorize clients and prospects into specific groups based on various criteria, such as industry, purchase history, or even event type.

With this data, you can easily pull up and view all members of a group, making it simple to tailor your marketing efforts. For instance, you can export these lists for direct mail campaigns or targeted email marketing.

CHAPTER 10

Benefits of Niche Marketing

1. **Higher Conversion Rates:** By focusing on a specific group, your marketing messages are more relevant and engaging, leading to higher conversion rates.
2. **Cost Efficiency:** Niche marketing is often more cost-effective than broad campaigns because it targets a smaller, more defined audience, reducing wasted effort.
3. **Enhanced Customer Loyalty:** By addressing the unique needs of each niche, you can build stronger relationships with your clients, increasing loyalty and repeat business.

Practical Steps for Implementing Niche Marketing

1. **Identify Your Niches:** Use your CRM to analyze your client base and identify potential niches. Look for patterns in your data, such as common industries or event types.
2. **Create Targeted Campaigns:** Develop specific marketing campaigns for each niche. This could include special promotions, tailored messaging, and personalized offers.
3. **Utilize Multiple Channels:** Reach out to your niches through various channels, including direct mail, email, and social media. Consistency across

all channels is key to reinforcing your message.

4. **Measure and Adjust:** Track the success of your niche marketing campaigns and adjust your strategies based on the results. This ongoing process helps refine your approach and maximize ROI.

Leveraging Marketing Tools

While the concept of niche marketing is straightforward, executing it effectively requires the right tools. For example, using email marketing tools with pre written templates for niche promotions can streamline your efforts.

Additionally, integrating third-party mail services to handle physical mailings can save time and ensure professional delivery.

Wrapping Up

Niche marketing is a powerful strategy for maximizing your catering business's potential. By focusing on specific client groups and tailoring your marketing efforts, you can achieve higher conversion rates, build stronger customer relationships, and ultimately increase your sales.

CHAPTER 11
THANK YOU NOTES

In college, one of my professors taught me the importance and value of sending a thank you note. It's such a simple gesture, yet it leaves a profound impact.

In today's fast-paced world, a handwritten thank you note is a rarity, making it as delightful as finding a surprise gift under the tree on Christmas morning. Sending these notes after a catering event builds loyalty like nothing else, especially when you've delivered exceptional food and service.

THANK YOU NOTES

The Power of a Handwritten Note

A handwritten thank you note stands out because it shows a personal touch and genuine appreciation. It's a small but meaningful way to say, "We value your business." At my restaurant, we made it a standard practice.

I had my office manager write them daily. Even if you're short on time, you can keep some note cards handy and jot them down while relaxing at home. It's these little details that clients remember and appreciate, fostering a sense of loyalty and connection.

Real-World Impact

The practice of sending thank-you notes not only strengthens client relationships but also sets you apart from competitors. In a world dominated by digital communication, a physical note feels special and personal. It shows that you've taken the time to acknowledge the client's choice to do business with you, reinforcing their decision and encouraging them to return.

Sending thank you notes is not just a nicety; it's a strategic business practice. It builds goodwill, reinforces positive impressions, and can even lead to word-of-mouth referrals. Clients who feel appreciated are more likely to become repeat customers and advocates for your business.

If Handwritten Isn't Feasible

While handwritten notes have the most impact, consistency is key. If you find it challenging to send them out regularly, consider using automated systems. For instance, automated thank you letters can be set up through catering software, with pre-designed templates that are sent to a third-party mail service for delivery.

This ensures that every client receives a note, even when your schedule is packed. With no minimums for mailing, this method allows you to maintain a personal touch without the logistical hassle.

Implementing Thank You Notes

1. **Set a Routine:** Decide on a regular schedule for sending thank you notes. This could be daily, weekly, or after every major event.
2. **Personalize the Message:** Even in automated notes, include a personal touch, such as mentioning a specific detail from the event.
3. **Use Quality Materials:** Choose high-quality note cards or stationery to reflect the professionalism of your business.

4. **Track and Follow Up:** Keep a record of sent notes and any responses. This helps in building stronger client relationships and tracking the effectiveness of your efforts.

Wrapping Up

A simple thank you note can go a long way in solidifying relationships with your clients. Whether handwritten or automated, these notes show that you value your clients and their business, fostering loyalty and encouraging repeat business.

Building on this idea of appreciation and rewarding loyal customers, the next chapter will explore the benefits of loyalty programs.

CHAPTER 12

LOYALTY PROGRAM

CHAPTER 12

Loyalty clubs have been around forever, with the earliest forms being simple punch cards. Airlines have perfected the art of loyalty programs with their frequent flier clubs, offering miles that can be redeemed for flights and upgrades.

Personally, I'm a big fan of Southwest Airlines; I carry two of their credit cards to turn everyday purchases into miles. This system has rewarded me with more tickets than I can use and a companion pass that allows a friend to fly with me for free.

These programs are powerful because they reward customers for their loyalty, encouraging repeat business.

The Concept of Loyalty Programs

Loyalty programs are about giving something back to your customers for their continued patronage. In the catering business, this can be a particularly effective way to build a strong, loyal customer base.

When I had my restaurant, we implemented a Pharm Rep Rebate Club, offering 5% of a pharmaceutical rep's net purchases back in gift certificates. This simple program not only encouraged repeat business but also created a buzz among the reps, turning them into loyal clients.

Creating a Successful Loyalty Program

The key to a successful loyalty program is to offer rewards that genuinely excite your customers. Whether it's discounts, free products, or exclusive offers, the rewards should be valuable enough to motivate continued patronage.

For example, in our Pharm Rep Rebate Club, we had one rep who saved up his rebates to pay for a family reunion. This kind of personal value reinforces the customer's decision to stick with your business.

Advanced Options

With today's technology, loyalty programs can go beyond simple gift certificates. One exciting option is to partner with services like Tango Card, which allows you to offer a wide range of electronic gift cards as rewards.

This is especially useful if you're targeting high-volume clients who might not want to use the same catering service repeatedly. Tango Cards provide flexibility, allowing customers to choose from various retailers, making the loyalty program more appealing.

Implementing a Loyalty Program

1. **Define Your Goals:** What do you want to achieve with your loyalty program? Increased sales, customer retention, or maybe a boost in new client referrals?
2. **Choose the Right Rewards:** Depending on your clientele, decide whether to offer discounts, gift certificates, or electronic gift cards like Tango Cards.
3. **Automate Where Possible:** Use software to track purchases and automate the reward process. This saves time and ensures consistency.
4. **Promote Your Program:** Make sure your clients know about your loyalty program. Use email campaigns, social media, and direct mail to spread the word.

The Impact of a Good Loyalty Program

A well-executed loyalty program can lead to double-digit growth in catering sales. It rewards your customers, making them feel valued and appreciated, and it gives them a reason to choose your services over competitors. Moreover, loyalty programs can serve as a unique selling point, differentiating you in a crowded market.

Wrapping Up

Loyalty programs are a powerful tool for building and maintaining a strong customer base. By offering rewards that excite and engage your clients, you encourage repeat business and foster long-term relationships.

CHAPTER 13

USING THIRD-PARTY DELIVERY SERVICES

In the fast-paced world of catering, one of the biggest challenges can be managing delivery logistics. You've got the food ready, the clients eager, but sometimes your own fleet of drivers just can't handle the load.

It's a good problem to have—demand outstripping your capacity—but it's a problem nonetheless. That's where third-party delivery services come in.

Why Consider Third-Party Delivery?

When your in-house delivery team is maxed out, leveraging third-party delivery services can be a lifesaver. Imagine you have a bustling Friday lunch rush, and your two drivers are already stretched thin.

You could miss out on additional orders simply because you don't have the manpower to deliver. With third-party services, this issue can be mitigated, allowing you to handle more orders without the stress of hiring more staff or investing in additional vehicles.

The Options: From DoorDash to Local Couriers

1. **DoorDash and National Providers:** Services like DoorDash, UberEats, and Grubhub have become household names. They offer broad coverage,

professional drivers, and established infrastructure. These platforms are convenient, but they do come with fees and commissions. However, they also bring a vast customer base, which can help increase your restaurant's visibility.

2. **Local Courier Services:** Sometimes the best solution is right in your backyard. Local courier companies can provide a more personalized service. They often offer flexible pricing and are more open to negotiating terms. These couriers can handle the overflow and can sometimes offer faster service since they know the local area well.

3. **Integrated Solutions with Burq:** For those looking for seamless integration, services like Burq can be a game-changer. Burq specializes in on-demand delivery, offering real-time tracking, and integrates smoothly with CaterZen's system. This means you can manage all your deliveries—both in-house and third-party—from one platform, streamlining operations and reducing the chance of errors.

Best Practices for Using Third-Party Delivery Services

1. **Choose the Right Partner:** Not all delivery services are created equal. It's crucial to vet your options. Look at their delivery radius, reliability, and customer service. You want a partner that will

represent your brand well.

2. **Set Clear Expectations:** Make sure to communicate your standards clearly. This includes handling food, delivery times, and customer interaction. Your brand reputation is on the line every time an order goes out the door.

3. **Manage Costs:** Be mindful of the costs associated with third-party services. While they can help you expand your reach and manage more orders, the fees can add up. Factor these costs into your pricing strategy to ensure you're still making a profit.

4. **Utilize Technology:** Integrating delivery services into your existing technology infrastructure, like using CaterZen's integration with Burq, can save you time and reduce errors. It allows for better tracking, reporting, and management of orders.

Wrapping Up

Using third-party delivery services can be an effective way to manage increased demand without overextending your resources. By choosing the right partners, setting clear expectations, and integrating technology, you can ensure that your customers receive the same quality service they expect, whether your own drivers or a third-party are making the delivery.

Remember, the goal is to maintain the high standards of

your catering business while maximizing your delivery capacity.

CHAPTER 14
REACTIVATION CALLS

CHAPTER 14

In the catering business, the ultimate goal is to create a perpetual cycle of repeat orders from satisfied clients. When a client orders from you once, you want to ensure they keep coming back, building a reliable stream of business.

However, sometimes clients go silent. Maybe they found a new supplier, or perhaps they just haven't had the need.

Regardless, it's crucial to have a system in place to reactivate these lost clients before they slip through the cracks completely.

The Importance of Reactivation

Reactivation is all about rekindling relationships with clients who haven't placed an order in a while. The value of this strategy cannot be overstated; it's significantly more cost-effective to bring back an existing client than to acquire a new one.

Plus, a returning client already knows and trusts your brand, making them more likely to place substantial orders or refer others.

Identifying Inactive Clients

The first step in a reactivation strategy is identifying who your inactive clients are. This typically involves:

1. **Tracking Order Dates:** Maintain a detailed record of when clients last placed an order. This can be as simple as a spreadsheet or as sophisticated as a CRM system that automatically tracks and notifies you of inactive clients.

2. **Defining Inactivity:** Determine what "inactive" means for your business. It could be 30 days, 60 days, or even longer, depending on your typical client order cycle. For example, if a corporate client usually orders catering once a quarter, reaching out after four months of silence might be appropriate.

The Reactivation Strategy

Once you've identified your inactive clients, it's time to reach out. The method of contact can vary based on what you feel would work best for each client. Here are some approaches:

1. **Personalized Emails or Letters:** A direct, personalized message can remind the client of the great experiences they've had with your service. Include highlights of past orders, new offerings, or special discounts to entice them back.

2. **Phone Calls:** Sometimes, a personal touch makes all the difference. A friendly call to check in can be the nudge a client needs to place another order. This also provides an opportunity to gather feedback on why they might have stopped ordering.

3. **Special Offers:** Who doesn't love a good deal? Offering a discount or a bonus item with their next order can be an effective way to encourage a client to return. This gesture not only re-engages them but also shows appreciation for their past business.

4. **Reactivation Campaigns:** Implement automated reactivation campaigns through tools like CaterZen's system. These can include scheduled emails or letters sent out after a certain period of inactivity. The advantage here is consistency and efficiency; you ensure every client gets a follow-up without fail.

Wrapping Up

Reactivating inactive clients is a critical component of maintaining and growing your catering business. By implementing a structured approach to reactivation, you can turn lapsed clients into loyal repeat customers.

Remember, the key is consistent communication and offering value that reminds them why they chose you in the first place. With a little effort and the right strategies, you can rekindle these relationships and keep the orders rolling in.

CHAPTER 15

MONTHLY EMAILS

January		
February		
March		
April		
Template Name	**Subject**	**Action**
April Fools Day	Free Steak and Lobster Lunch for the Office	+ 🗑 A ✉
Tax Day	Important Tax Information Included	+ 🗑 A ✉
Admin Professional's Week	Make an Executive Decision with (TYPE IN YOUR COMPANY NAME)	+ 🗑 A ✉
Tax Season	Make Life Less Taxing with (TYPE IN YOUR COMPANY NAME)	+ 🗑 A ✉
Spring Cleaning	Grab your mop and broom!	+ 🗑 A ✉

In the digital age, staying connected with your catering clients is more important than ever. An effective way to keep your business top of mind is through regular email communication, specifically with a well-crafted electronic newsletter.

These monthly emails can be a powerful tool for maintaining customer relationships and driving repeat business, but they must be handled with care to avoid becoming a nuisance.

The Purpose of Monthly Emails

Monthly emails serve multiple purposes:

1. **Staying Top of Mind:** By regularly appearing in your clients' inboxes, you ensure that your catering business is always considered when they need services.
2. **Promoting Special Offers and Events:** Use these emails to announce special deals, seasonal menus,

or upcoming events. This can encourage clients to book more frequently and try new offerings.

3. **Educational Content:** Share tips, recipes, or catering advice that showcases your expertise. This not only provides value but also positions your business as a helpful resource.

Best Practices for Email Frequency

It's crucial not to overuse this permission-based medium. Sending too many emails can lead to high unsubscribe rates or cause your messages to be marked as spam. The sweet spot is generally one to two emails per month. This frequency keeps your audience engaged without overwhelming them.

- Once a Month: This is a safe frequency to maintain regular contact without being intrusive.
- Twice a Month: If you have frequent promotions or updates, a bi-monthly schedule can work. However, ensure that each email offers distinct and valuable content to the reader.

CHAPTER 15

Crafting Your Emails

When it comes to the content and design of your emails, there are a few key points to consider:

- Personalization: Whenever possible, personalize your emails. Use the client's name and reference their past orders to make the communication more relevant.
- Engaging Content: Your emails should not just be sales pitches. Include useful content like catering tips, behind-the-scenes stories, or staff spotlights.
- Clear Calls to Action (CTAs): Whether it's to book a catering service, try a new menu item, or attend an event, make sure your emails have clear and compelling CTAs.

Wrapping Up

Monthly emails are a vital part of your marketing strategy. They help keep your brand top of mind, encourage repeat business, and build a deeper relationship with your clients. By following best practices and leveraging tools like CaterZen's email marketing system, you can create effective and engaging communications that not only inform but also inspire action.

Remember, the key is consistency and value. By delivering useful, interesting, and relevant content, you can ensure that your clients look forward to your emails, rather than seeing them as just another item in their inbox.

CHAPTER 16

DAY AFTER FOLLOW UP
CALLS - 1-3-5-7

The importance of follow-up in the catering business can't be overstated. A successful event doesn't end when the last guest leaves; it's followed by the crucial task of checking in with your clients.

This chapter is all about mastering the art of follow-up calls, ensuring you not only meet but exceed your clients' expectations, leading to repeat business and long-term relationships.

The Power of the Day-After Call

The day-after call is a simple yet powerful tool in your customer service arsenal. It shows clients that you care about their experience and are committed to delivering top-notch service. By reaching out the day after an event, you can gather valuable feedback while the experience is still fresh in their minds.

This immediate follow-up can help you:

1. **Gauge Client Satisfaction:** Ask open-ended questions about how the event went. Were there any issues? What did they particularly enjoy? This feedback is invaluable for continuous improvement.
2. **Address Any Issues Promptly:** If there were any hiccups, this is your chance to make things right. Whether it's a late delivery or a missing

DAY AFTER FOLLOW UP CALLS - 1-3-5-7

item, addressing the problem quickly can turn a potentially negative experience into a positive one.

3. **Strengthen the Relationship:** A genuine check-in builds rapport and shows that you value their business beyond the transaction. It's about building trust and demonstrating reliability.

The 1-3-5-7 Call Formula

A highly successful caterer once shared a golden follow-up formula: the 1-3-5-7 call schedule. This involves making follow-up calls after the first, third, fifth, and seventh orders. Here's why it works:

- **First Call:** This initial follow-up sets the tone for your client relationship. It's your opportunity to ensure everything went smoothly and to express your gratitude.
- **Third Call:** By now, your client has a good feel for your service. This is a great time to solicit deeper feedback and discuss any additional services they might be interested in.
- **Fifth Call:** This call helps cement the relationship. By this point, you should be familiar with your client's preferences and needs, allowing you to tailor your services more closely to their expectations.
- **Seventh Call:** By the seventh call, the relationship should be well-established. This is the perfect time

101

to explore loyalty programs or offer exclusive deals to encourage continued patronage.

Managing Follow-Ups Manually

To effectively manage follow-ups manually, start by creating a comprehensive log, either in a spreadsheet or a physical notebook, where you can record essential details such as client names, contact information, event dates, and notes from follow-up conversations.

Setting reminders is crucial, whether you use a calendar, sticky notes, or alarms on your phone, to ensure you make timely calls.

After each interaction, update your log with the discussion's outcomes and any required actions, keeping a consistent record to track progress. Regular reviews of this log will help you stay on top of client needs and maintain strong relationships.

Leveraging Technology for Efficiency

While manual tracking is effective, it can be time-consuming and leaves room for error. Utilizing technology, like CaterZen's software, can streamline this process by automating reminders and centralizing all client interactions in one system. This ensures no follow-up is missed and allows you to manage your client relationships more efficiently, freeing up time to focus on delivering exceptional service and growing your business.

Wrapping Up

The day-after follow-up call is not just a courtesy; it's a strategic move that can set your catering business apart. By consistently reaching out to clients, addressing their concerns, and showing appreciation for their business, you foster a loyal customer base that will keep coming back.

Remember, the real money in catering isn't in one-off events—it's in building a herd of happy, repeat clients. So, pick up that phone and start dialing—it's time to lock in those repeat orders!

CHAPTER 17

REFERRALS

CHAPTER 17

Think about the last major purchase you made—whether it was a gadget, a car, a vacation destination, or even a restaurant choice. Chances are, you relied heavily on recommendations from friends, family, or trusted colleagues.

That's the power of referrals. What people say about your business carries a lot of weight, often more than any advertisement could. For a catering business, this word-of-mouth marketing can be an invaluable asset.

The Importance of Asking for Referrals

The most straightforward way to generate referrals is simply to ask. Many satisfied clients are more than happy to recommend your services, but they might need a little nudge.

Whether through a letter, an email, or a quick phone call, asking for referrals should be a regular part of your follow-up process. It's a simple yet effective way to expand your client base without much effort.

Creating a Referral System

To maximize the impact of referrals, it's essential to implement a structured referral program. At CaterZen, we believe in systematizing the referral process to ensure consistency and effectiveness. Here's how you can do it:

1. **Referral Rewards:** Offer your clients a tangible incentive to refer to your services. This could be a discount on their next order, a gift card, or even a percentage of the catering sales generated from their referral. The reward size can be adjusted based on the client's value to your business.
2. **Communication Strategy:** Regularly remind your clients of the referral program through your marketing channels. This can include emails, printed materials, or even a section on your website. Make sure the process is clear and straightforward for your clients to refer to others.
3. **Tracking Referrals:** Implement a tracking system to ensure that referrals are properly credited. Each referred client should receive a unique code or mention the referrer's name. This way, you can accurately track the source of the referral and reward the original client accordingly.

Wrapping Up

Referrals are one of the most powerful and cost-effective ways to grow your catering business. By asking for referrals and implementing a structured system to encourage and reward them, you can turn your satisfied clients into your best salespeople.

CHAPTER 17

Remember, every happy customer is a potential advocate who can bring in new business. So, don't be shy—ask for those referrals and watch your client base grow!

REFERRALS

CHAPTER 18

BRINGING IT ALL TOGETHER

Congratulations on reaching the culmination of this guide!

By now, you've gained invaluable insights into strategies that can significantly boost your catering business's efficiency and sales. If you implement even a fraction of these tactics, you could see a 10-20% increase in your sales.

But the best part? You don't have to do it all manually. CaterZen brings these strategies together, offering a comprehensive suite of tools that streamline your operations, improve client communication, and automate many of your business processes.

The Comprehensive Benefits of CaterZen

CaterZen isn't just software; it's an all-in-one solution designed to tackle every aspect of your catering business. Let's walk through how CaterZen can support each of the key areas discussed in this book:

1. **Effortless Inquiry Handling:**
   - **Tools:** Catering Inquiry Web Forms, integrated CRM for lead management.
   - **Benefits:** Captures detailed client information upfront, ensures timely follow-ups, and maximizes booking potential.

BRINGING IT ALL TOGETHER

2. Email Marketing:

- **Tools:** WYSIWYG Editor, pre written templates, targeted campaigns.
- **Benefits:** Streamlines client communication, maintains engagement, and drives repeat business through automated, professional email campaigns.

January			
February			
March			
April			

Template Name	Subject		Action
April Fools Day	Free Steak and Lobster Lunch for the Office		✚ 🗑 A ✉
Tax Day	Important Tax Information Included		✚ 🗑 A ✉
Admin Professional's Week	Make an Executive Decision with (TYPE IN YOUR COMPANY NAME)		✚ 🗑 A ✉
Tax Season	Make Life Less Taxing with (TYPE IN YOUR COMPANY NAME)		✚ 🗑 A ✉
Spring Cleaning	Grab your mop and broom!		✚ 🗑 A ✉

3. Event Space Management:

- **Tools:** Online booking interfaces, detailed event calendars.
- **Benefits:** Prevents double bookings, streamlines scheduling, and enhances client service with easy-to-manage event details.

4. Robust CRM (Client Relationship Management):

- **Tools:** Centralized client profiles, automated task reminders, segmentation.
- **Benefits:** Personalizes client interactions, tracks preferences and history, and facilitates targeted marketing efforts.

113

Michael Attias

Selected Customer:	Restaurant Catering Systems (10% Discount)	Highlighted Notes for Michael Attias
Michael Attias start new order		Food Allergy — Michael has a gluten allergy
First ordered on: Jun 12, 2018	1415 Straighway Avenue	Call Note (11/09/2018 @ 10:54 AM) — Needs Wedding Proposal
Orders to date: 27	Nashville, TN 37206	Call Note (05/18/2018 @ 3:57 PM) — He didn't answer. Call back.
Total spent: $17,857.78	p: (615) 831-1676 ext. 101	Add a note for Michael Attias
Most recent order: Aug 09, 2024	m: (615) 969-7090	
	f: Not Specified	
	e: Michael@caterzen.com	

5. Streamlined Financial Management:

- **Tools:** Automated invoicing, sales receipts, accounts receivable management.
- **Benefits:** Ensures timely payments, reduces manual errors, and enhances cash flow management.

Description	Rung Up/Collected	Payments on sales from 2024-08-01 - 2024-08-21	
Catering Sales		Credit	$60.00
Food Sales	$8,725.38	Square Payment	$350.00
Beverage Sales	$0.00	Cash	$600.00
Liquor Sales	$0.00	Deposits Applied	$30.00
Paper Goods	$0.00	CATERING TICKET 1: Outstanding / Unpaid	$7,546.73
Equipment Rental	$0.00		
Catering Items Sales Subtotal	$8,725.38	**Payments on sales from before 2024-08-01**	
Service Fees	$243.19	Credit	$6.00
ezCater Sales Tax	$0.00		
Other Sales Tax	$584.37		
Grand total sales tax (ezCater – Other)	$584.37		
Third party remitted tax	$0.00		
Delivery Fees	$320.00		
Coupon/Discount	-$28.94		
ezCater ezRewards Program	$0.00		
ezCater ezDispatch Charge	$0.00		
ezCater Fees	$0.00		
ezCater ezCaterer Service Fee	$0.00		
Total Amount	$7,849.96		
Tips	$264.75		
Total Amount With Tips	$8,106.73		
Catering Deposits	$380.00		
House Charge Payments	$6.00		
Grand Total Rung Up/Collected	$8,494.73	**Total Payments**	$8,494.73

114

6. Empowering Your Sales Team:

- **Tools:** Integrated phone module, marketing and collections calls module.
- **Benefits:** Improves lead follow-up, enhances communication tracking, and automates sales tasks.

Select any options to filter your contacts (or leave blank to select all contacts)

Include only these locations:	Choose Locations
Belongs to any of the selected groups:	Choose Groups
Last call outcome was any of:	Choose Outcomes

Select one filter to further refine your contact list

☐ Has an invoice that is more than:	25	days overdue (based on today's date)		
☐ Has a birthday in date range	08/19/2024 📅	Until	08/25/2024	📅
☐ Has an upcoming event in date range	08/21/2024 📅	Until	08/28/2024	📅
☐ Has a previous event in date range	08/14/2024 📅	Until	08/21/2024	📅
☐ Has an order scheduled in date range	08/19/2024 📅	Until	08/25/2024	📅
☐ Reached milestone of 5 orders within the date range	08/19/2024 📅	Until	08/25/2024	📅
☐ Minimum number of days since last order (based on today's date) 90				
☐ Has never placed an order				

7. Efficient Multi-Location Management:

- **Tools:** Unified system, tiered menu pricing, centralized CRM.
- **Benefits:** Maintains consistency across locations, optimizes resource allocation, and simplifies data management.

8. **Streamlined Delivery Management:**
   - **Tools:** Delivery Manager, automated route planning, Burq integration.
   - **Benefits:** Ensures timely deliveries, optimizes routes, and enhances client satisfaction.
9. **Online Ordering:**
   - **Tools:** Customizable online ordering platform, integrated payment options.
   - **Benefits:** Increases convenience for clients, boosts sales, and reduces order-taking errors.

10. **Never Miss a Follow-Up:**
    - **Tools:** Quote reminders, rebooking reminders, CRM integration.
    - **Benefits:** Ensures consistent follow-ups, maximizes booking opportunities, and enhances client retention.

11. Simplify Your Kitchen Operations:

- **Tools:** Recipe management, inventory tracking, electronic and printed production reports.
- **Benefits:** Streamlines kitchen tasks, reduces waste, and ensures consistent quality.

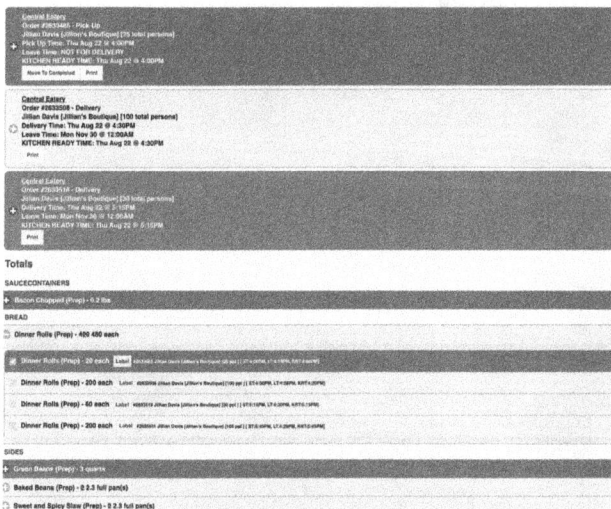

12. Seamless Integration with Third-Party Services:

- **Tools:** Integrations with QuickBooks, Google Calendar, payment processors.
- **Benefits:** Streamlines operations, reduces manual data entry, and enhances overall efficiency.

13. Crafting Winning Proposals and Quotes:

- **Tools:** Automated proposal creation, customizable templates.
- **Benefits:** Impresses clients, reduces preparation

time, and ensures clear communication of services.

14. Simplifying Billing with Invoices & E-Signatures:
- **Tools:** Automated invoicing, e-signature integration.
- **Benefits:** Speeds up the billing process, ensures legal compliance, and enhances cash flow.

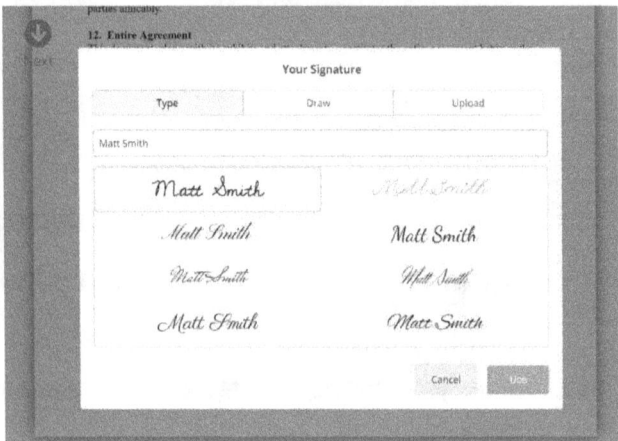

15. Building Client Loyalty with Reward Programs:
- **Tools:** Automated loyalty and referral tracking, personalized rewards.
- **Benefits:** Encourages repeat business, enhances client satisfaction, and drives word-of-mouth referrals.

16. Maximizing Efficiency with Integrations:
- **Tools:** Comprehensive integration options

(Chowly, Tango Card, Nearby Now, etc.).

- **Benefits:** Centralizes operations, enhances data accuracy, and provides a unified view of business activities.

The CaterZen Promise

CaterZen not only simplifies these processes but also pays for itself through enhanced operational efficiency and increased sales. By automating routine tasks and providing tools that streamline every aspect of your business,

CaterZen allows you to focus on what you do best—delivering exceptional catering services.

In a competitive market, CaterZen provides the edge you need to not only meet but exceed your clients' expectations. Whether you're managing a single unit or multiple locations, CaterZen offers scalable solutions that grow with your business.

Final Thoughts

Our goal at CaterZen is to help successful caterers become more successful. We will turn your catering chaos into calm.

CHAPTER 18

Any one of these seventeen "Catering Multipliers" can help you grow your catering. Added together they can cause your sales to soar.

Whether you do it yourself or use our catering software to make it more systematized, turning your back on these strategies will cost you lost sales you'll never get back.

If you would like a free, no obligation trial or demo of our software, please visit www.CaterZen.com. We would love to explore the profitabilities of working together.

To Your Catering Success!

Michael Attias
President/Founder
CaterZen Catering Software

www.ingramcontent.com/pod-product-compliance
Lightning Source LLC
Chambersburg PA
CBHW071207200326

41519CB00018B/5416